ONE AT A TIME

By Caroline A. Wolff

as told to Nancy L. Quatrano

WC Publishing

an On-Target Words company

ISBN-13:978-0-9854381-8-0
ISBN-10:0-9854381-8-5
Also available as a Kindle book, and for all other e-reader devices.

Copyrights @ 2013 by Caroline A. Wolff

Copy Edits by C. Konrad, and J. Peters

Cover design: Akira007-fiverr.com

Cover photo leased from Dreamstime.com

Interior layout and design by Nancy Quatrano

Printed in the United States of America

All Rights Reserved. No part of this book may be reproduced, stored in a retrieval system, or transmitted in any form or by any means, electronic, mechanical, photocopying, recording, or otherwise, without written permission from WC Publishing.

All these stories are real. However the names of the St. Gerard residents have been fictionalized to protect the students and their families.

WC Publishing, an On-Target Words company
4625 Cedar Ford Blvd.
Hastings, FL 32145
www.ontargetwords.com
nancy@ontargetwords.com

What People Are Saying...

What a wonderful uplifting group of short stories. And what a very special place St Gerard's Campus is. To have saved so many girls and babies is truly a gift from God. I highly recommend this very, very special book. You will want to read these heartwarming stories that will indeed touch your heart and soul. I for one will be contributing to this wonderful organization.
- Judith Leigh, Author of *A Father's Hope* and *When the Vow Breaks*

This is a wonderful account of how the Wolff's have helped many lives, not only the girls but their unborn children at the time the girls entered St Gerard. I have been truly blessed to read these stories.
- Cheryl Johnson-Konrad, Beta reader

This clearly shows that when God wants something big done, He taps everyday people to do it. We can all make a difference if we'll just say, "Here I am, Lord."
- Lynn Kathleen, Author of "Merciful Blessings"

Table of Contents

From the Editor i

From Carol Wolff ix

IN THE BEGINNING 1

CROSSING PATHS 7

MICHELE 11

COLEEN 17

THE TALL KID 24

HALEY 27

JACEY 35

DESTINY: Little girl lost 40

ARIANA 43

ABIGAIL 46

MELISSA 49

RUTH 60

EVA 65

MAGGIE'S BABY 68

HAPPILY EVER AFTER 72

POPE JOHN PAUL II..75

APOSTOLIC BLESSING 78

MYSTERIOUS WAYS...79

From the Editor

Dearest Reader,

The word "catholic" means universal. The word Catholic, with the capitalized "c" refers to a specific Christian denomination.

I assert that the defense of life and dignity is a *universal* human concern and responsibility, not a Catholic one, or even an American one, specifically. This book isn't about a religion or a nation, but it *is* about God, Jesus Christ, and the mother of Christ. And, it is about the decision to protect life as opposed to destroying it.

And though Catholic's may be the

denomination that pays the most honor and respect to Mary, the mother of Jesus Christ, I've yet to meet *anyone* who disagrees that Mary was and is His mother, whether they are Catholic or not.

I make these distinctions to set the context for reading these powerful and touching stories. Because of the actions spurred on by the faith and beliefs of one battered family, thousands of lives have been saved, and thousands more have been positively impacted. A priest once mentioned during a time of discouragement, that one life saved will result in millions being saved by Judgment day.

A read through the Holy Bible reveals how the Lord has always sought out those who feel they were least equipped to carry out seemingly impossible missions: David, a young shepherd boy, killed Goliath, a giant of a man, and later led the nations of Israel as their king. Daniel, an ordinary Jewish boy, became mentor and tutor to kings, even to the point of facing death in the lion's den and walking out unscathed. Noah, a drunk and spiritually weakened man, was chosen to build an ark that saved humankind; Moses stuttered horribly and yet was chosen to speak for an entire people; Ruth, a humble Gentile (non-Jewish) woman with a pure heart was chosen to secure the lineage that later bore Jesus Christ into the world. The stories go on and on, but the scenario is much the same.

Jesus chose the humblest of men and women to teach his message of love. He ate with the lowly on a regular basis, not the upper crust.

And so it was with Carol and Al Wolff in the 1970's. Their upper-middle class home was turned upside down when a trusted friend embezzled all of the money in their business, leaving them broken-hearted over the betrayal, responsible to care for trusting customers out of their savings, and ultimately bankrupting them mentally, physically and spiritually. With three teenage children still at home, and several other homeless teens to care for, they moved to a new place and started all over again. Al became a carpenter and Carol, a teacher. Neither of them could see the blessing in all of the humiliation and agony of those years. They were hard, mentally, emotionally and spiritually. (This story and others are told in Carol's memoir, *Tell the Children*.)

Out of the humblest beginnings, God calls us to action. Some of us get easy assignments, others not so much. Carol was charged with saving children. All the children she encountered. And then—the children of *those* children if necessary.

And so, St. Gerard's Campus in St. Augustine, Florida was founded to provide a safe, fully accredited high school that would allow teen mothers to complete their education *and* care for their children. To learn about the love of the Lord and the gifts of His son, Jesus Christ, and to choose life for their babies instead of abortions. A large percentage of grads have gone on to careers in the scientific, medical, and business communities. And most importantly, more than 31,000 babies celebrate birthdays who would not be alive today if not for St. Gerard's.

St. Gerard's Campus depends 100% upon donations. No government or religious organization supports the school. They run a full-service adoption counseling service. They answer the phone all day and night, 24/7. The teachers are all highly educated and committed to making a difference in the world, one teen at a time. The students are taught life skills along with their academic, theological, and child-rearing courses; they can do a budget, balance a checkbook and know how much a loan is really going to cost them.

The stories contained in this book are true. And the book was written to show the world that God is most definitely still alive and well, even in this age of rampant hopelessness and distress.

The glory of God is always present when people reach out to help one another, in whatever way they can, be it with prayer, money, time or talent. And, perhaps you'll even begin to see that the mission of Christ's mother Mary, to teach us to stand for the dignity of all life, from time of conception through the time of transition off this mortal coil, is *also our mission*, as given to us by her son Jesus.

So, thank you for reading this book. We hope you'll share it and talk about it. We hope you'll find it in your heart to support St. Gerard's and other programs in your community that stand tall for the rights of all those who cannot stand for themselves.

The Lord promises to bless us in accordance with the blessings we have been to others. May God bless you richly in this life as well as the next.

Nancy Quatrano

From Carol Wolff

St. Gerard Majella, a Redemptorist missionary, is the patron saint of expectant mothers. Like the St. Gerard who was canonized in 1904, the St. Gerard Campus stands to protect the mothers and babies who arrive here.

There are thousands of stories from St. Gerard's, each one as different as the women and girls themselves. Most endings are happy, some are not. But for each and every woman that walks through the doors of the St. Gerard Crisis Pregnancy Center, no matter who she is or what she needs, she is treated with all the dignity and respect that she deserves.

Thousands of women come through the doors every year, from all ages, every ethnic background, economic tier, and religion. For those contemplating abortion for whatever the reason, our degreed and licensed counselors are ready to help them make a good decision and give life to their babies.

We have adoption counseling and many qualified families waiting with loving homes for a child of their own. We're there every step of the way to assist the birthmother with her choice and all the care she needs.

Sometimes it's a young couple that's looking for help. They're delighted to be having a child of their own, yet they're terrified to tell their parents. Our counselors get involved there as well. They are taught what makes up a loving, strong home for their family, and how to go about making it happen. Healthy families are a child's greatest asset.

Most pregnant teens are outcasts in the mainstream high school setting, so we offer the girl and her family the chance to enroll in our accredited high school to complete her education. Some teens are abandoned by their families, so we arrange shelter and counseling for the young girls. In addition to being a licensed Day Care facility, St. Gerard is also a licensed foster care facility.

For the young people who come to us, in addition to pregnancy testing and sonograms, we provide baby and adult clothing, food, furniture and resources, all offered with a great deal of love, and without discrimination or charge.

We always need financial assistance, so donations of any size are always greatly appreciated. But we need volunteers, too. Maybe being a driver or receptionist is of interest to you, and the donation of your time and talent would be appreciated.

Whatever you can do to help us to continue to make a difference in the lives of these young women is a blessing. Visit our website at www.stgerardcampus.org for more information.

I hope you enjoy this collection of true stories. May the Lord bless you generously.

Carol

IN THE BEGINNING

In Carol's book, TELL THE CHILDREN, she tells the story of how she found herself involved with helping women and children in the St. John's county area.

Back in 1981, shortly after she and her husband Al had relocated to St. Augustine, Carol met a teenage mother who'd been put out of the house by her parents and who had taken refuge with an abusive man. When the man broke the infant's jaw and the teen mother called her for help, Carol knew something had to be done, not only for that young woman, but for all the young women who would find themselves in that situation. Carol took custody of that teen mother and baby and helped them get on their feet because there were no other resources back then. And, she knew that it was only the beginning.

Between 1981 and 1984 when they incorporated, Carol and Al had to learn what it would take to open, fund, and operate such a place. They turned to Beta House in Winter Park for guidance, information and support.

Beta House was a shelter located in a former abortion clinic that had been purchased by two women: one Jewish, one Catholic. When Carol approached them with her ideas for St. Augustine, the women were happy to teach her what they could about obtaining grants and operating a successful shelter.

They referred her to the Edythe Bush Charitable Foundation and counseled her to find an older building that wouldn't be too costly to buy and repair, but could also serve as collateral going forward. Al, who was then in real estate, located the building on Route 1, which although not in great condition, was perfectly zoned for what they wanted to do. It had been a rehab center for people with addictions and the basic layout seemed suited for a residential center with daycare facilities.

While Beta House had 19 grant writers on commission, Carol was the one to learn to write the grants in the early days. Mentored by Mr. Lee , she learned to develop operating and building budgets, to keep to those budgets, to obtain grants and to run the center like a business. She was told to hire a CPA and to plan for future repairs and expenditures.

Beta House had a clinic, pregnancy testing center and a residence, but Carol wanted St. Gerard campus to look just a little bit different. Her years with displaced teens had taught her that they needed a home-like environment more than anything, so that's what she had in mind when they began their renovations.

As she knew the Lord would, He provided the down payment for the building, just in the nick of time. The Foundation presented Carol with a check for the initial $100,000 to make the purchase, and when her budgets and plans were in place, they provided additional funds to help with the renovations, too. Carol began to learn the ropes of serious fund-raising.

Instead of dorms, residents at St. Gerard have their own room and bathroom. Each mom and baby have their own place to live and care for and each student has a study area, as well. They share kitchen and laundry facilities and they take turns drawing up grocery lists, budgets, and doing the cooking and cleaning in the kitchen. The goal is not only to make the girls feel at home, but to teach them how to manage a home of their own.

Mr. Lee and Mrs. Bush are now gone, but never forgotten and always missed. Their commitment, knowledge, and generosity have changed the lives of young women throughout central and northern Florida. And, as things work in this world, the ripple effects of their influence can probably be felt worldwide.

In the twenty-eight years since the doors of St. Gerard opened, Carol, Al and the staff of St. Gerard have helped rescue and guide girls and young women out of poverty, dependency and welfare. The women learn to cope, with faith-filled assurance, to rise above their circumstances and grow into loving, capable mothers, productive members of society and positive forces in the workplace. They leave with their full high school diploma and plans for college degrees. Many obtain academic scholarships.

In the beginning was one young mother and one

baby. Since then, Carol and staff have mentored more than 48,000 mothers and supported the birth of nearly 31,000 babies.

CROSSING PATHS

The mission of St. Gerard Campus is multi-faceted, but centers around the concept that abortion is wrong: it not only stills the heartbeat of an unborn child, it can often kill the spirit and soul of the mother, too.

Every year, St. Gerard and local churches sponsor the Walk for Life, a celebration of life and a call to all people to stand up for the sanctity of all life.

ONE AT A TIME

Dr. Alveda C. King, niece of Dr. Martin Luther King, and Caroline Wolff met once, then committed to standing shoulder to shoulder for the 20th pro-life weekend (February 2008) held in St. Augustine, Florida. King, a mother of six and a grandmother as well, delivered the keynote address as well as other speeches throughout the weekend. Having experienced the heartbreak of abortion in her own life, she was passionate about the topic.

> "This is the day to choose life. We must live and allow our babies to live. We must end the pain of post-abortion trauma. If the dream of Dr. Martin Luther King Jr. is to live, our babies must live. Our mothers must choose life. If we refuse to answer the cry of mercy from the unborn, and ignore the suffering of mothers, then we are signing our own death warrants."

Wolff, mother of five, grandmother and great-grandmother, founded St. Gerard to provide a safe, loving, instructional home and school environment that supported single mothers in choosing life for themselves and their babies. The majority of the graduates are successful mothers and have gone on to advanced degrees and careers as doctors, nurses, dentists, hospital technicians, teachers and all levels of professionals. Some of them had nowhere else to go. They were put out on the street and urged to get abortions. More than 31,000 babies can be thankful that their moms chose to make the right – although very difficult – decision to have them.

The cards, letters, phone calls and photos that cover the walls at the campus are a testimony to the relationship that Carol Wolff developed with the students of St. Gerard Campus over the years.

MICHELE

Michele was being raised by her parents in rural Florida. While in high school, she fell for a young man being raised by a foster family.

As so often happens, Michele and her young man conceived a child and all of a sudden a large variety of problems loomed on her horizon.

Her grandfather, shotgun in hand, decided one evening to "convince" the young man to marry his granddaughter, but there was one problem. The boy was in the foster care system, a minor, and he could not lawfully marry Michele.

Her grandmother, terrified that her husband just might shoot the young man, called St. Gerard's in a panic. Carol Wolff, director and founder, directed her husband Al, to get the Sheriff's department out there fast, and proceeded to talk to the grandfather in an attempt to diffuse the situation.

When the Sheriff's deputies arrived, they were able to remove the shotgun, calm down the grandfather, and everyone agreed to work for reasonable solutions.

Michele dreamed of going into law enforcement when she graduated high school, but being pregnant, she feared high school was impossible for her, and but for the St. Gerard

Campus, it probably would have been. At St. Gerard's, she finished high school, learned to care for herself and her baby, and applied and was accepted to college.

While her family supported her as well as they could, Michele and her boyfriend still wanted to marry. After much investigation, Carol realized, that if Michele's mother adopted the young man out of the foster care system, she could give him permission to marry Michele.

And so it was, that Michele married her beau, who was then her legally adopted brother. Bizarre perhaps, but it was a solution to a very complex matter. Too young, with too many hills to climb perhaps, but they stayed together and had another baby.

Then, Michele became pregnant with child number three. The idea of another child was more than she could bear. Too little money, too many little mouths, dreams she feared were not strong enough to endure all the stress led Michele to make the decision to abort her third child, despite the pleas of her young husband not to do it.

Having been educated and nurtured at St. Gerard's, Michele knew her decision was not a good one. But at the end of her rope, as is the case with many women who seek out abortions, she felt there was no other choice for her.

As Michele waited in the abortion center, determined to end her baby's life, she heard the voice of the Lord.

"Don't take my baby's life," He said.

She ran out the door of the clinic into the arms of the pro-life prayer partners outside the building, and begged them to pray for her. For all of them. The other women left the clinic that afternoon with their babies as well.

Did the Lord use this country girl to save the lives of His gifts? To energize the men and women who constantly pray for an end to abortions? It would be just like the Lord to do that very thing.

***

Years later and many young women and babies later, Carol called the Sheriff's department to respond to a domestic situation.

Two deputies arrived on the scene: one female and one male. With deep compassion, warm understanding, and quiet resolve, the female deputy was impressive. As Carol turned to leave the location, the deputy called out to her.

"Miss Carol, you probably don't remember me, but you made a huge difference in my life." She stepped forward, one hand resting comfortably on her utility belt. "I'm Michele, your guardian angel."

Not only had she gone on to achieve her dream of going into law enforcement, she'd excelled in it. Her partner that day smiled when he pointed out that Michele was one of the finest deputies on the force.

Of course she is! That's exactly how the Lord works.

COLEEN

New Jersey 1960's

Coleen lived down the street from the mental institution in Blackwood, New Jersey. And, her mother struggled with psychiatric issues. One of the Wolff boys really liked her a lot, and she was a best friend of one of the Wolff daughters, too. She was around the house a lot.

One night Carol was at the supper table and became very concerned about her. She left the family eating dinner, got in her car and drove to the church in Blackwood, only to find Coleen inside the church, huddled in a pew, crying her eyes out. A suitcase sat beside her.

"What's wrong?" Carol asked. She knew she could never leave her at the church.

"My mother and I had a horrible argument. I can't reason with her, so I packed my bag and here I am. I have no idea where I'll go."

"Well, you know you can come stay with us, right?" Carol said.

She laughed through her tears. "But you already have so many kids living there."

"So what? It's all right. One more won't make any difference, honey. We'll figure it out - but you can't stay here. Will your mother be more angry if you come stay with us?"

Coleen shook her head. "No, she just wants me out of the house. I don't think she really cares where I go."

And so, Coleen came home to join the many others at the Wolff residence and became one of the "kids." She finished high school and enrolled in the community college, so Carol and husband Al bought her a little car to get back and forth to school.

But Coleen had a ministry all her own from the time she was sixteen years old. She enlisted the aid of several of the other kids and they volunteered at the Blackwood Mental Hospital, a former tuberculosis center. After school, Coleen would stop in to see if she could help anyone there and on Sundays, the kids would get the elderly patients in their wheelchairs and take them to mass in the chapel. The hospital housed chronically ill patients who were dependent on ventilators, as well as juveniles, the elderly, and the mentally ill.

Father Jim, the priest who ministered to the patients, was as upset as Coleen was, at the horrible conditions in the hospital.

"Miss Carol, if I bring them to task about the conditions these patients are in, they'll throw me out of here and there won't even be a mass to go to. But you're a civilian - maybe you can do something about this?"

So Carol recommended that Coleen take careful and precise notes of what she witnessed at the hospital.

Coleen took the notes and then Carol, her family, and all the kids in the youth group spent a good deal of time in prayer. When a group of people pray together for something to change, it's amazing what God comes up with. Carol decided to take her findings to Rutgers in Camden, and present them to the law students there to use as a case study.

An in-depth investigation was eventually launched and those results made the front pages of newspapers in several states, for weeks. The hospital was ultimately closed, and several people who were unjustly incarcerated by family members, were released.

That young teenager with a big heart and a fire inside to serve the Lord by caring for those who couldn't care for themselves made a huge difference.

Sound a little like the story of David and Goliath? It sure does to me.

***

Coleen went on to college, got her master's degree in social work, and ran a variety of programs in the Hammonton area for the migrant farm workers there. She married a migrant worker who was an addict at the time, but who has since come to know the Lord and is clean as a whistle. They've been married so long, she speaks with a Spanish accent and that's her *second* language.

She calls Carol monthly to check on her "flaky friend" as she calls her. She remembers when they would do silly things just to find laughter in the hard days.

Carol says of herself, that she's always been something of a big kid. Last time they spoke, Coleen was talking about retiring from the NJ Division of Youth and Family Services, so she could open her own practice to council Christian couples with marriage difficulties.

THE TALL KID

One day at the St. Gerard Campus, a tall, good looking young man stood at the front desk.

"Can I help you?" the volunteer receptionist asked.

"I'd like to speak to Miss Carol," he said.

"Can I tell her what it's about?" the woman asked.

"It's kind of personal," he said.

As the volunteer used the intercom to let Carol know someone had asked to see her, an older woman came through the door and stood with the young man.

Carol, thinking her visitor was probably someone needing money for something or other, put aside her work and walked through to the lobby.

The woman spoke first. "Nineteen years ago, you argued with me for one hour to save his life. And here he is."

"I love my mom," he said. "I'm so proud of her and you know, she's raised fifty-five other teenage boys."

Amidst the hugs and tears and smiles, Carol didn't write down her visitor's name because everyone in the room was stunned into a humble silence.

Before Carol and Al had their children, the Blessed Mother chose Carol to help save the children. All of the children.

Especially the unborn.

HALEY

Haley arrived at St. Gerard house by way of a case manager. She'd been in the foster care system, but pregnant teens can't stay in the foster care system, so the obvious solution was to see if Haley could fit in at the St. Gerard Campus.

Carol had a room available at the time and welcomed Haley to the group, but Haley was almost inconsolable. For her, it was worse than being put into jail. She cried and cried for days, hold up in the room she'd painted a very "special" color – a bedroom that is still known as "Haley's" room.

"I want to leave, Miss Carol, I don't want to stay here," she cried.

Carol knew that Haley had been bounced from one foster home to another and St. Gerard's probably seemed like just another stop in the system. So Carol, who was committed to helping Haley get acclimated, get her education, and make good decisions for herself and her unborn child, called the baby's father.

He begged Haley to stay with Carol to get the help and support she needed because she was only seventeen and he couldn't take care of her. He urged her to get her education finished and graduate, and then they'd make their plans for the future.

Haley stayed and began to nest in the hot-pink room. In just a short while, she took on the role of an older sister to many of the teens at St. Gerard's. She helped them with hair and homework, and coached them on dressing and behaving like educated young women. A bond was formed that would be tested, but never broken.

As the year went on, Haley brought her boyfriend to St. Gerard's and he made Carol a promise that if she ever needed Haley's help with anything, that he would make sure Haley was there.

Before they could marry however, her future father-in-law had a stroke and became severely disabled which left five minor children at home without an able-bodied parent. Haley swore that she would never let those children be separated or put into foster care, and so she committed to make a stable, clean and loving home for them all. Now the scared teen of just a year before, was taking on the responsibility for five minor children, her own infant, her disabled soon-to-be father-in-law, her fiancée, and herself.

In a panic, she called Carol to let her know that they didn't even have any furniture in the house and asked what in the world she could do about making a good home without furniture. And in that request, Carol saw God at work, again.

Carol had just received a call from a friend who closed their business in St. Augustine. They were leaving all of their new, modern furnishings behind and closing the restaurant immediately so they could fly back to California. Carol and Al supervised as Haley and her fiancé loaded all of the furnishings onto a big trailer. Bedroom sets, dishes, towels, sheets, glassware, appliances, you name it, they got it! The chef, whose life was so disrupted by the failure of the business told Carol he was happy to know that such a big family was going to benefit from his loss.

Through their relationship at St. Gerard's, Haley considered Carol something of a surrogate mother so they talked on a regular basis, and the young woman became a staunch advocate for St. Gerard's.

Haley dedicated herself to taking care of their house, the children, and her college work as well as her job so that her fiancé could stay home to care for the baby and his younger siblings.

ONE AT A TIME

Shortly after Haley's second child, her fiancé's sister became addicted to drugs, which left more another child without a healthy, able parent. So, in addition to the seven that Haley and her fiancé were already caring for, they added another for a total of eight children from ages newborn to seventeen.

Out of Haley's commitment to keep all those children out of the foster care system, she and her fiancé built a healthy, solid home for everyone. She learned to budget and plan healthy meals. She studied hard and qualified for money to go to college. He managed the children and made sure they all had outings, exercise and adventures.

Carol remembers when Haley came to St. Augustine from Ocala, to have her staples removed after delivering her second baby. Haley appeared at the campus to show "Miss Carol" her new baby, instead of going back home to Ocala right away. Carol was as proud as any mother could be, for Haley's new child and for who Haley had become.

Haley has finished her college now and she's working as a CNA to support the remaining family. She loves nursing and enjoys working, even though she decided to breastfeed her last child because it was an experience she didn't want to miss and she'd decided not to have any more children.

She and her fiancé have just married, the fall of 2013. After the wedding, she's planning to have all the children baptized at one time. That should require nearly as much planning as the wedding did!

An abandoned, terrified, hysterical seventeen year-old was transformed into a mature young woman who made it all happen for herself and her family – that's the amazing work that God does through St. Gerard's.

JACEY

Jacey came to St. Gerard's when her mother was in jail. The remaining family threw her out. She had ADD and it was a challenge to get her to stay with schooling, but she did. The largest challenge was that she couldn't sit still, so during class she'd get up and wander around the room, even though she was listening. It was almost painful for her to sit for very long, but it drove the teachers crazy. Carol spent a lot of time smoothing things out for her.

Jacey didn't have much in the way of a support structure. Her mother was in jail, and her father raised pit bulls. Her grandmother couldn't help her. St. Gerard's was all she had. The baby's father wanted nothing more to do with her but when he did see her, he was abusive, hoping she'd be too scared to file for child support.

She had a beautiful little boy that would never leave the school without poking his head into the office to wave at "Miss Carol."

But after the relationship with the father of her son ended, she fell in love with another man and became pregnant with twins. So, there she was, a mother to a toddler and pregnant with twins. She needed St. Gerard's, but would it be a good fit for her?

Carol had her tested through a variety of programs. Jacey was bright and had a good IQ, but her emotional state left her easily agitated and highly vulnerable. The teaching staff looked for ways to teach her the programs and still have control in the classroom. Carol spent a lot of time mediating between Jacey and the campus teaching team.

One of the things that needed to happen, was Jacey needed support for her oldest son. St. Gerard's helped her to get legal counsel to assist with getting the father to come to court so they could reach an agreement. During her pregnancy and while trying to learn her studies, she was called into court four times with the father of her firstborn. Ultimately, the court decided that Jacey and the boy's father would share custody equally, so she would only have her son every other week.

Saddened by what seemed to be an unjust decision, she worked to graduate and have healthy twins. Despite the stress and challenges, Jacey carried her twins full term! She and her fiancé are planning to marry and after that, they will go back to court to petition for visitation and custody that will benefit her oldest son.

Jacey realized that she had to let go temporarily so that she didn't add any more stress to the lives of her children, but with the support of her fiancé, she's looking forward to winning the next custody battle for her son.

At St. Gerard's, she learned courage, strength and faith, characteristics that were there all along because the Lord put them there. They just needed a bit of nurturing.

And a generous sprinkling of faith.

DESTINY: Little girl lost

A defiant and determined young woman, Destiny came to the school pregnant and facing many challenges. But her determination set her apart from the others on our campus that year.

She was an above-average student who loved to learn, regardless of the topic. She always pushed herself to learn more than was required, and in 2006, she gave birth to a lovely baby girl and graduated St. Gerard's High School, with honors.

She entered St. John's Community college, receiving a Pell Grant and a Bright Futures

Scholarship to help with college. She took time from her busy schedule as a full time student and mother to visit St. Gerard's and speak to the current students, encouraging them to work hard and keep trying.

Destiny found that college didn't offer the challenges that she needed, so she enlisted in the U.S. Army. With her father's promise to care for her daughter, she worked hard and became a specialist E4 in weaponry. In 2008, she was deployed to the Middle East as a computer specialist in charge of nuclear weapon release for her battalion. To ensure that her daughter would be protected while she was gone, she agreed to give her father custody.

After being deployed for a year, Destiny returned home to St. Augustine, only to find her father and her daughter, gone. Though her father remarried after Destiny left the states, and he stopped by St. Gerard's with his little "buddy" to visit, he never let on that he was leaving the area permanently.

Destiny's mission now is to find her beautiful baby girl and fight to get her back. But Destiny knows how to fight now, and she knows how to trust the Lord to get her through the challenges. She's paid a terrible price for her service to this country, a price that many of our service men and women pay—the loss of their homes and families.

Carol says that she'll always keep Destiny and her daughter in her prayers. And if there's one thing the people at St. Gerard's have a lot of faith in, that's the power of prayer.

ARIANA

Sometimes life throws so much at a person, it would seem impossible they would survive at all, let alone excel. And sometimes, when people get to witness that kind of courage, it has the power to change many lives.

Ariana was a resident in the dorm. A beautiful African-American teen, she had sickle cell anemia, and she was pregnant. Despite her battle with a disease that is often fatal, she gave birth to a lovely baby girl, and graduated St. Gerard's with honors.

Ariana is a woman of great faith. She adores her daughter, has gone on to obtain four college degrees, including her Bachelor of Science in pathology. In four years, she suffered four strokes, yet she carries on as though she's invincible.

She's returned to the Run for Life more than once, and just an hour after she spoke to the crowd in 2012 about keeping faith and preserving life, she was admitted to the hospital for a blood transfusion. Even as she was being treated, she offered comfort and strength to others.

"Don't you worry one minute about me. I know that God's going to take good care of me," she told Carol in the hospital.

From abandoned and challenged, to being a champion for the unborn, Ariana is a shining example of what love and dignity can do for another human being. She's an inspiration to all about what can be done in the knowledge that God is in charge of our life.

He doesn't promise easy, only that He will be with us every step of the way to lift us up.

ABIGAIL

She was fifteen years old and had run away from home. Many times. Her mother, terrified and frantic, finally located her living on the streets with a drug dealer.

Her mother and grandmother brought her to the campus from another state where her mother lived. Her grandmother, a St. Johns County resident, knew she couldn't control her or provide a safe place for her, so they thought St. Gerard's might be the answer.

When she arrived at the campus, she was one tough kid. Angry, stubborn, and without an ounce of trust in any of the staff, including Carol, she was ready to run back to the streets at the first opportunity. She was like an untamed stallion, always ready to bolt. She wasn't going to be told how to live, by anyone.

She used language that would make a stevedore blush, and she lied and stole in hopes that she'd be thrown out of the program. But Carol and the team refused to give up on her. Their commitment to help every single girl that comes through the door meant that Abigail would not be an exception.

The teen was on the phone with her boyfriend, every time she could sneak away. With a constant barrage of prayers, and the diligent work of one of the St. Gerard's certified counselors, the young woman eventually realized that life on the streets with a cocaine addict wasn't such a great career path.

Today, at eighteen years of age, Abigail has a beautiful baby girl, graduated St. Gerard's High School, works a part time job, and is enrolled at St. John's College to further her education.

Almost 90% of the graduates of St. Gerard Campus go on to college or some other secondary education. When people are allowed to learn to be capable, they will always excel.

MELISSA

A priest from Jacksonville called Carol and asked her to place a young pregnant mother. She'd been hiding in the attic of her boyfriend's house and she was very far along in her pregnancy.

The priest and the young mother's family feared that the boyfriend would continue to hide her, or maybe even run away with her, but he had no resources to make sure she got the medical support she might need being pregnant so young.

Carol agreed to take Melissa into the program. She lived in the dorm with the other girls, and one day during dorm inspections, a hypodermic needle was found under the mattress on Melissa's bed.

Carol's instincts told her that Melissa was a good person, with a good moral compass, even though she was making some very bad choices at the time, so she gambled on being honest with the girl. Melissa told Carol it was her boyfriend's needle, and Carol replied that it didn't matter, having paraphernalia in the dorm was grounds to be removed from the program. She suggested that Melissa's parents come in for a consultation and then the four of them would decide the outcome.

Melissa's mother was a psychiatric nurse in denial about her daughter's situation. Melissa was sure she wanted to marry this young man, and her father was about to lose his mind with worry about her. The last thing he wanted her to do was marry a "drug-using loser".

After several conferences, and once Melissa was doing well with her studies, she began to settle in at the campus. Carol wanted Melissa to see her boyfriend for what he really was, so she arranged for the two of them to spend some time together.

"Melissa, tomorrow's Saturday. How about we go do something fun? You're working hard, some fun would do everyone good. I'll pick him up in Jacksonville, take you guys to Marineland, give you a chance to discuss your future together. See how he really feels, what his plans are."

Melissa was uncertain at first, especially since she knew he stayed out all night and wouldn't be happy about an early outing, but as Carol continued to talk, the young woman got excited about her day out with the father of her baby.

"Operation Rescue has job openings, right here. He could come live with a good foster family in this area, come over here to the campus to finish his schooling, then work with the on-the-job training team and learn a trade," Carol offered.

Convinced that her beau was indeed a man who would step up and be responsible for caring for her and the baby, Melissa looked forward to a great day.

At seven the following morning, they arrived at the boyfriend's house in Jacksonville, but he didn't answer the phone and wasn't waiting outside the house. Melissa got out of the car, and climbed over the fence, then marched into the house to get him.

They stood on the front porch while he complained about being rousted so early. It was obvious he'd been sound asleep. Around his neck hung ear buds and on his hip was a music player.

"Where did you get that?" Melissa asked him.

"I bought it last night," he said.

"And do you have money to buy us lunch today? Or did you spend it all?" she asked.

Carol chimed in. "Don't worry about lunch. I'll treat you both, today. Let's get going."

As they drove south toward Marineland, Carol talked to the young man about participating in the Operation Rescue program.

"I've got a really good job lined up for you, some wonderful people to live with, and you can come over to the school and take some courses that will help you in the construction business. How's that sound?"

"Wow man, that means I have to go to work?"

Melissa poked him in the ribs. "Yeah. Did you say we were going to get a place together and raise the baby? How can we do that if you don't work?"

"Well, then I can't go to the mall at night. That stinks. This is really pretty heavy stuff," he complained.

Carol was convinced that the young man hadn't left home without some kind of dope on him, so she opened the car windows and let the wind ruffle his long hair. When she glanced into the rearview mirror, she noticed a thin white stick placed behind his ear.

"Give me that joint, right now," she said, reaching behind her with one hand. "I don't need to get stopped with that in my car and get busted. Give it up."

"Oh man, you can't take my stuff. We were going to smoke it later."

Carol pulled over to the side of the road and turned to look at him. "Are you crazy? She's pregnant! She can't be smoking pot or anything else. Now give it to me."

Reluctantly he handed it over and Carol tore it into tiny bits and let it fly out the window.

When they arrived at Marineland for their day of fun, the boyfriend was depressed at the idea he should be responsible for his child and girlfriend, and Melissa was crushed, because now she could see that everyone was right about him.

Carol gave them money for lunch, and told them to call when they were ready to be picked up. Melissa called a few hours later.

"Miss Carol, we're pretty tired. Can you come get us now?"

"Find a bench in the shade and rest. I'll be there in a little while," Carol said. She figured a little more time together might do them both some good, so she took her time getting there.

They were very sullen when they climbed in the car.

"Okay, we'll get you back to Jacksonville. Just relax and enjoy your last hour or so, together," Carol said.

On the long drive back, Melissa realized she had no future with the young man, and told him so. When Carol dropped him off at home and got

Melissa back to campus, she hoped that they'd heard the last of him.

That wasn't to be the case, though. A short time later, he called Melissa and told her if she didn't come back to him, he was going to kill himself.

Hysterical at the thought he would do that, Melissa went to Carol. Carol called the same priest who had brought Melissa to St. Gerard's and filled him in.

"We can't take a chance and ignore this. If he's serious and we did nothing, it would be a horrible shame," she explained.

The priest, who knew the young man for a long time, promised Carol that he'd go right over and check on him. He called Carol later in the afternoon.

"You know, I've known this young man since he was in grade school. I spent the better part of the afternoon with him. He isn't going to hurt himself. And, he promised he would get off the drugs, get a good job and support his child."

Carol let Melissa know the outcome and everyone was relieved, but Melissa knew she couldn't count on him. With the support of the staff and her parents, she graduated High School and went on to get two nursing degrees, one of which was the same as her mother's: Bachelors of Science in Psychiatric Nursing.

In June of 2013, eighteen years after Melissa was at the St. Gerard campus, Melissa's father called to tell Carol how grateful he was for all that had been done for his daughter. He'd read a recent article in the Jacksonville newspaper about the campus and it spurred him to call.

God uses all sorts of things to get us moving. A newspaper article, a pregnant daughter, a cancer diagnosis. Each journey is different.

And each journey will have big challenges. It's good that the Lord promised that we don't have to handle any of them alone.

That's what St. Gerard's is all about.

RUTH

Two religious groups got together and brought Ruth to St. Gerard's to finish school. The daughter of a Caucasian-American father and a Korean-born mother, her disgrace was more than her mother could ignore. Ruth's mother beat her with a belt.

The evidence of the beating was on Ruth's face, where the buckle had cut her cheekbone and left a horrific bruise. It wasn't safe for her to live at home with her parents. Her father loved her and wanted her home, but he couldn't take care of all her needs at the time, so he supported her in relocating to the St. Gerard campus.

She was doing okay with her high school studies, but she was still in love with the father of the baby, and they planned to get married and have a life together. However, he was an African-American and his mother forbid him to marry a Caucasian girl; Ruth's father forbid her to marry the young man because he felt he was trouble.

Ruth had her baby and wrapped her in a lovely handmade blanket donated by a volunteer. The blanket meant more to Ruth than any of the St. Gerard staff would know for years.

She finished school and won a full scholarship to play basketball and get her college education. But she decided to defer the scholarship and take off with her boyfriend. Lo and behold, Carol received a call from Ruth and she was abandoned in a small desert town on the border of Mexico. Her boyfriend had been selling drugs and finally just disappeared one night.

She was broke, alone, and had the baby with her, so Carol paid her way to Jacksonville and called Ruth's father to let him know she was safe and coming home.

It was some time later when Carol got a call from Ruth's father who told her Ruth was going to the University of Gainesville on that athletic scholarship and a grant for expenses. Everyone at St. Gerard's was delighted and relieved at Ruth's decisions to come home and get her education so she could care for herself and her daughter.

In 2010, Carol was contacted again by Ruth. She'd married a fine young man who had adopted her little girl as his own. She finished college with a degree in physical therapy, and now lives in Hawaii. She and her husband own a boutique and she's pretty much a stay-at-home mother.

And, she never forgot St. Gerard's or the beautiful handmade blanket that made her feel loved and special. She planned a trip back to St. Gerard's to offer the students courage and inspiration by sharing her story. But she promised Christmas gifts, as well.

A handmade blanket was given to every girl on the campus in honor of the lovely person who had made one for Ruth's baby girl; and she gave Carol a check for $15,000.

"When my mother died, she left me some money," Ruth said. "I figure, you guys can always use some money."

Carol said a truer statement was never made. The campus can always use money. And the funds were put to good use helping the newest group of girls who needed a helping hand in life.

What goes around, does come back around. Love shared with one, is love shared with many.

EVA

Eva was sixteen years old, pregnant, still in high school and scared to death. So, in the winter of 1987, she moved into the dorm at St. Gerard Campus.

Twenty-five weeks into the pregnancy, she discovered she was having twins. Four weeks later, her premature sons were born.

From sunup to sundown, Eva was on the run. Studying and visiting her babies at the Jacksonville hospital kept her busy. And her dream to get an education and provide well for her sons was her motivation.

"...Without the St. Gerard [Campus] I wouldn't have been able to do it," she confesses. "They not only gave me an education, they helped me stay focused."

Today, the twins are twenty-five years old and leaders in the community. Chris works in law enforcement and John is an EMT and firefighter. They both shrug and smile and readily admit they just like helping people.

"Nobody thought I could do it or if these kids could grow up to do anything for the community." Both, Eva states, "have become great young men."

Carol and the St. Gerard staff knew that Eva could succeed. They are delighted and proud of her and her two sons, but they aren't really surprised.

Success is the outcome for many of the young women who come through the doors of St. Gerard Campus.

MAGGIE'S BABY

The baby was released from the hospital three days after his birth. His head was enlarged and he cried all the time. The hospital said the baby was fine, if not a bit fussy. But after several days of non-stop crying, Carol ordered the baby to be taken to Wolfson Children's Hospital for another opinion.

The baby had several broken bones and the mother was accused of child abuse, but Carol didn't believe that the young woman had hurt the baby, so she arranged a lawyer for Maggie.

The court ordered Maggie and her newborn to reside at St. Gerard Campus full time, under full time supervision by the staff. This meant that the Campus had to provide supervision seven days a week, all day and all night. During the school year and during the summer. A staff member was required to sleep in the same quarters as the mother and child, without exception.

Maggie was devoted to her little boy and diligently performed the physical therapy ordered by the doctors to help her baby heal and develop. Day after day, she'd call out to Carol and the house mother to come see the new accomplishment of her infant son. Though behind others his age, the little one learned to roll over and in time, sit up, smile and respond to verbal stimuli.

The court order also allowed the father supervised visitation rights. Maggie and her son were allowed to visit him at his parent's home every weekend for a few hours, but in time, the restrictions became too much for their relationship and the mother and father ended their courtship.

Despite what were later diagnosed as developmental disabilities, the child grew, learned coordination, and became a more normal, active baby boy. Amazing what that amount of commitment can do, isn't it? Maggie's commitment and the commitment of St. Gerard and the staff to give Maggie and her little one a fighting chance.

When Maggie dropped by to visit Carol and the staff earlier in 2013, Carol was delighted to see that the little boy who was almost left behind, was sporting a great haircut, a warm and infectious smile, and looked and behaved like a regular three year-old boy. She asked that her story – her miracle – be included in this book.

God doesn't tell us life will be easy. He does promise that He will give us all we need to take care of His people. Maggie and her son are indeed among His people!

HAPPILY EVER AFTER

It takes a lot of money to see to all the needs of the students, the babies, the buildings, the staff, the volunteers, the vehicles and well, just about everything.

Carol and Al still spend a good deal of time working on raising funds. They take no salaries and put in many hours. They attend dinners and functions to discuss the needs of the community and the students at St. Gerard. They make thousands of personal phone calls to remind people of pledges and promises and to ask if they can do more when donations are down.

In addition to the annual golf outing that is generously sponsored by A1A Aleworks, the fundraiser that garners the most attendance and support is the Annual St. Gerard Luncheon and Fashion Show, held at the Renaissance Hotel in World Golf Village every December.

In addition to the plaid-clad toddler models, some with blonde curls and dark eyes, the 2012 event became the wedding day for Taylor and her fiancé , Edward. When the models had completed their turns on the runway and lunch had been cleared, Edward's grandfather, a Baptist minister, performed the marriage ceremony.

Why the Fashion show? Mr. And Mrs. Williams told reporters that it just wouldn't have been complete without the St. Gerard family being there.

POPE JOHN PAUL II

In the 1960s and 1970's, Carol and Al ministered to homeless teens in the Camden, New Jersey area. One such young man was named Barry. He was a serious-minded, reverent fellow who had decided to become a priest.

He was, for the most part, tormented for his goals and his demeanor, but he would not be swayed. Carol and Al remember times when they'd taken all the kids camping and canoeing and Barry was thrown overboard from the canoe or the girls would hug and kiss him relentlessly.

When Barry completed high school, he entered the Pauline order in Cherry Hill, New Jersey. After he was ordained, Carol shared a dream with him.

"I dreamed of a large stained-glass window with beautiful roses all over it. I'm sure it was in Rome," she told him.

"I've always dreamed of seeing Rome, though I doubt I ever will," he told her. "If I do though, I'll look for the window."

Years later Barry revealed to Carol during a phone call, that he'd seen that very same stained-glass window in Rome! At that time, Barry was the Secretary General of the Pauline order, which was a very intensive and powerful position to hold. He asked Carol if there was anything he could do for her and Al or St. Gerard Campus.

"I'd like to have a full Papal Blessing," she told him. He assured her it would be done.

Before he could secure Pope John Paul's blessing however, Barry was shipped back to the United States. He was not without friends in Rome though, and he arranged for a fellow priest in Rome to secure the Blessing for St. Gerard.

On October 7, the feast day of the Holy Rosary, in 1996, Pope John Paul II imparted his Apostolic Blessing to the staff and members of the St. Gerard home and school. It was to be a day of prayer and commitment to stop abortion.

The Blessing still hangs today in the offices at St. Gerard, a constant reminder that the work going on there is truly blessed.

ONE AT A TIME

APOSTOLIC BLESSING

The Holy Father
John Paul II

paternally imparts
his Apostolic Blessing to

Staff and Members of the
St. Gerard Home and School,
on the feast of the Holy Rosary,
7 October 1996 a day of prayer and
commitment to stop abortion.

MYSTERIOUS WAYS

In all the years that I've worked with children, I've seen all sorts of miracles, some disguised as heartaches, others just plain, out-in-the-open miracles. I wrote about many of those in my spiritual memoir, TELL THE CHILDREN.

This book, for the most part, records some of the more visible, easily measured miracles that I've been privileged to witness while at St. Gerard Campus.

In closing, I have two connected stories to share with you. One has to do with the commitment and power of a specific organization in the Catholic church known as the Knights of Columbus. Knight organizations are made up of Catholic men, active in their faith, who work together with priests, in prayer, time and talent, to make life better for the world.

For nine years, my husband Al and I attended the First Friday Adoration prayer vigil held at the Cathedral in St. Augustine, on behalf of all unborn children. For some years, we prayed all night from dusk until dawn, in the company of Knights and priests who took turns hourly coming to the chapel to pray, do readings, or chant.

(After some time, the Bishop changed the

vigil to a daytime event as keeping those late hours got harder and harder on those of us who were getting up in years but still wanted to do it.)

Anyway, Al would deliver each Knight's prayer to their offices so that every hour on the hour, they could come into the chapel prepared with their set of prayers.

The hours between 3 A.M. and 4 A.M. were the hardest to stay awake and focused, so Bishop Snyder would join us and pray along with us to help sustain us. One Friday night, he looked around and noticed how few priests were present in the chapel.

"You know Carol, the priests are sleeping and we are here. They should be here, too."

I laughed and shook my head. "Father, those are your kids. I have enough of my own."

He laughed and laughed. "You have a point there."

Which goes to show that though we take our mission seriously, our Heavenly Father also gives us a sense of humor to get us through the dark hours.

One night we were at the vigil and my beeper went off which would happen if one of the girls had an emergency. One of the resident's was in labor and she had to be air lifted to Shand's in Jacksonville.

We got to the hospital as quickly as we could, and though the young mother was stable and out of danger, her three pound son was not.

We kept vigil with our young mother who didn't want to leave her little one. So one evening as I sat looking at the tiny baby with medical tubes, equipment and lines sticking in him everywhere, he looked back at me. And for some time, he just looked at me with such sadness, my heart was just about breaking. I could almost hear him telling me how unhappy he was.

I sent the exhausted mom to the cafeteria to get something to eat and when she left, I got up, went to the little one and put my hand gently on his forehead. I prayed to the Lord and the Holy Mother and asked them for grace on the baby. Then I closed his tiny eyelids and he went almost instantly to sleep.

In a matter of minutes he had gone home to the Lord and when his mother returned, he was already peacefully gone. Her tears of sorrow at his passing were mixed with gladness that his time of suffering was over.

Leaving God in charge doesn't mean we don't mourn the loss of our loved ones, it just means we let Him do what is best for everyone. He's a god of love and we have faith in that fact.

Now as heartbreaking as it was for that young girl to lose her sick baby, God worked good things out of it all.

The pediatrician needed someone he could trust in his home to help with the children and household while he did his practice, which at that time included house calls. The young woman found a home, a purpose, training, and support during a very hard time in her life. She was led to pursue a career in medical administration at the Mayo Clinic as a result of her time with the doctor and his family.

A young pregnant girl was delivered from despair and hopelessness and led to a life of great happiness and accomplishment.

The way may certainly seem to be mysterious to us, but we are no mystery to the Lord who loves us with a passion.

HOW CAN YOU HELP?

There are a lot of ways that you can help the St. Gerard Campus and the preservation of life! The first and most important way, is to remember them in your daily prayers. Say a Rosary or pray a Novena on our behalf. We firmly believe that every life is sacred and to be respected, and that we can change the world with our prayers, if they are heartfelt. So, remember the girls and babies at the campus, as well as the teachers there.

Pray for their families. And, pray for changes in the world that will recognize the sacredness of all life: the unborn, the poor, the handicapped, the elderly and the incarcerated.

There are tangible ways that you can help St. Gerard Campus. Those include donations of your time, your talent and your money! Volunteers are needed for a variety of important functions. You might want to remember St. Gerard's in your will or estate planning. Donations to St. Gerard Campus are completely tax deductible. And, you might want to buy additional copies of our books to share with friends and family members!

For information regarding helping the Campus in any of the ways mentioned above, please contact St. Gerard Campus, and ask to speak with the Dean or Director. The phone number is 904-829-5516. Or, visit www.stgerardcampus.org.

If you are interested in using this book as a fundraiser, or in selling this book in your retail establishment and would like to learn about discounted bulk pricing that includes shipping and handling, please contact WC Publishing by sending an email to Nancy@ontargetwords.com. The largest portion of the profits will directly benefit St. Gerard. The young women – and the bills — keep coming in every day.

Thank you for taking a stand for the sacredness of human life!

WANT MORE???

Read true stories about the miracles in Carol Wolff's life that led to her founding the St. Gerard Campus, where **every** life is sacred! She has been directed by the Holy Mother and visited by our Lord, Jesus Christ—and though an ordinary woman, she's been led to help accomplish amazing things.

Just like *One at a Time*, *Tell the Children* is available at St. Gerard Campus, Kindle, Kobo.com and Amazon.com, or ask for it at your favorite bookseller! Books purchased through St. Gerard will be autographed.

Bulk sales with discounts can be arranged for both books. Email Nancy@ontargetwords.com

Softcover ISBN: 978-0-9854381-7-3

Made in the USA
San Bernardino, CA
12 January 2015